Don't Call Mommy at Work Today Unless the Sitter Runs Away

Mary McBride
with *Veronica McBride*

Illustrated by Christine Tripp

ⓜMeadowbrook
Distributed by Simon & Schuster
New York, New York

Library of Congress Cataloging-in-Publication Data

McBride, Mary.
  Don't call mommy at work today unless the sitter runs
away.

    1. Working mothers — United States — Psychology.
2. Work and family — United States. 3. Children of working
mothers — United States. I. McBride, Veronica. II. Title.
HQ759.48.M23   1988   306.8'7   87-34709
ISBN 0-88166-112-0
ISBN 0-671-66402-6 (Simon & Schuster)

ISBN 0-88166-112-0 (unpriced)

Illustrated by Christine Tripp
Edited by Patricia McKernon

Copyright ©1987 Mary McBride

Published by Meadowbrook, Inc.
18318 Minnetonka Boulevard
Deephaven, MN 55391.

BOOK TRADE DISTRIBUTION by Simon & Schuster,
a division of Simon and Schuster, Inc.
1230 Avenue of the Americas
New York, NY 10020.

S & S Ordering: 0-671-66402-6 (priced)

88 89 90 91 10 9 8 7 6 5 4 3 2 1

Printed in the United States of America

Contents

Chapter 1

Once upon a Time Card

You've overwatered vine and fern.
The kids complain you're much too stern.
Boredom makes your spirit yearn.
Don't hang around—go out and earn!

One reason so many women are joining the work force.

Each year the percentage of married women who work increases. By the time this book gets into readers' hands it could be between 99 and 100 percent.

Why are so many women joining the work force? One woman put it succinctly: "It beats running away from home." But there are many other reasons for working. Recently a questionnaire was sent to women who work outside the home asking why they decided to get a job. Here are some of the answers they gave:

"I found I was discussing current events with the baby."

"I wanted some pleasant 'Good mornings' instead of surly ones."

"I wanted to be able to get a drink of water without having to get drinks for two or three other people."

"I wished I could walk in the door and say 'I'm home!' "

"I wanted to be in an *adult* car pool."

"I wanted to eat lunch with people who don't have elbow fights."

"I wanted to take my husband to a party where *he* didn't know anyone."

"I wanted to hear jokes that weren't knock-knock jokes or riddles."

As you can see, working has its advantages. Work offers many other benefits that you might not have considered. For instance, you can avoid doing volunteer work by saying "I'd love to help but I don't have the time." Some other benefits of working include:

You can buy new clothes without feeling guilty.

When someone comes to your door collecting for charity, you can say "I gave at the office."

At teachers' conferences, you can end complaints about your kids by saying "I'm on my break—I've got to get back to work."

2

You can get co-workers to buy the things your kids are selling.

The noise of office machines may help you be able to stand your teenagers' music.

You will suffer many hardships when you join the paid work force. You'll have two jobs instead of one, you'll have to buy expensive labor-saving appliances, and a baby-sitter will raise your child. But look on the positive side. You'll learn to be better organized, you'll be able to afford a microwave, and your sitter might teach your two-year-old to say yes.

Chapter 2

Don't Have Anyone under Ten Proofread Your Resumé

If in telling your age
The truth you've denied
You can write in (Approx.)
So you've not really lied.

One of the most important steps toward getting a job is preparing a resumé. This involves gathering together all the information that will make you seem valuable to an employer . . . without lying.

Some employers are tenderhearted, so you might want to convey the message that you *need* a job. Using a faded typewriter ribbon will not achieve this effect. However, you could bracket your children's names and write "all needing orthodontia" beside them.

Here are more suggestions for writing a successful resumé:

Prepare your resumé while your children are fighting. You'll be much more motivated to get a job.

For references, list people to whom you owe money. They'll do everything they can to see that you get hired.

If you're copying a resumé from a book, make sure you don't use the same name, education, experience, and references.

Put down Q for your middle initial. Someone might call you to find out what it stands for.

List cooking as a hobby. Employers might think you'll bring delicious treats to work. Also list cross-country skiing and snowshoeing as hobbies so they'll think you'll get to work in the worst weather.

Under "Health Problems," write *workaholic*. Do not list *pierced ears* under "Surgery."

List any special talent you have, such as "Can charm people so they aren't upset by being put on hold." However, do not write "Can always manage to look busy."

When you finish your resumé, put it in your metal safety box to protect it from jelly and chocolate.

If you don't have a typewriter that beeps when you mis-spell a word, proofread your resumé carefully. A mistake will

Some achievements are better left off your resumé.

automatically land yours in the pile marked "Don't call us; we'll call you."

Here are some other things to avoid in writing a resumé:

Don't pepper the paper with exclamation points to show how enthusiastic you are.

Even though your home resembles a war zone, don't check "Military Service."

If you attach a picture, be sure you're not winking.

When listing previous employment, don't go back as far as your first Kool-Aid stand.

Never lie about your weight on the resumé. Many jobs require a physical and you'll be found out.

Even if you were in every club in high school, resist the urge to cut out your yearbook picture and activities list and paste them on the resumé.

Do not list any of these items under "Education":
Played with educational toys as a child.
Read books my mother brought home from the library.
Watched "Jeopardy."
Watched "Sesame Street" with my children.

After you've polished your resumé into a literary masterpiece, you'll have to get it into the hands of an employer who needs your skills. Be resourceful and imaginative, but don't go too far. No matter how anxious you are to get a job, don't go around parking lots putting copies of your resumé under car windshield wipers.

Chapter 3

Don't Tell Them How Much You Need the Money

Should I wear a suit
Or just a dress?
Oh, how can I make them
Tell me yes?

You will probably receive a number of letters in response to your resumé submissions. The first paragraph will compliment you, but the second paragraph will begin with *however* and say that you are overqualified, underqualified, or that someone else was more qualified.

You might feel discouraged if you think "I'll never get a job," so try a little innocent self-deception. Tell yourself that sending out resumés *is* your job—that way you'll work at it every day.

When you finally get called by an employer, try a few of these suggestions for a successful interview:

Wear gloves—they absorb the sweat from your palms.

If you are told you're overqualified, offer to burn your diploma.

If the prospective employer is taking notes while interviewing you, imagine he or she is doodling.

Wear gloves. They absorb the sweat from your palms.

Attempt to find a common relative. Many employers practice nepotism.

Make sure your baby-sitter doesn't call you during the interview.

Books on interviewing often cover what to do in an interview, but few give an extensive list of things *not* to do, such as chewing gum and showing pictures of your children. Other interview taboos are:

Don't tell them how much you need the money.

Don't tell them how much your baby-sitter needs the money.

Don't show them your furniture catalog with circled items.

Don't say "Can we start over?" halfway through the interview.

Don't ask if you can tape the interview so you'll be better at it the next time.

Don't ask for your resumé back to use again.

Don't ask if you can sit in on other candidates' interviews.

Don't ask "Who's the best so far?"

Don't ask if you should call the newspaper and cancel the ad.

Don't go back to your interviewer for directions if you get lost leaving the building.

Remember: if you don't get hired, you can't sue the store where you bought your interview outfit. But if you do get the job, celebrate! This is a big step. Maybe you won't be on "Lifestyles of the Rich and Famous" next week, but your financial health will definitely improve. Just think: you won't get hysterical anymore over a run in your panty hose.

Chapter 4

Just One Chocolate Sprinkle on My Cone, Please

Lose weight before you start your job.
Just simply make a vow:
At the picnic you'll wear shorts
And make them all say "Wow!"

If you feel like the woman who took an office job and said she looked like a Hardy in a roomful of Laurels, perhaps you should lose a teensy bit of weight. Look on the positive side. Losing weight has its benefits. For instance, you can spend more time with your children; ask them to hold down your legs while you do sit-ups.

Perhaps it isn't your fault that you're overweight. Maybe you've been given a greater love of food than the average person. You'll know this is the case if after touring your new place of employment all you can remember is where the vending machines are.

Look for indications that your "No thank yous" were exceeded by your "My, that does look goods." A few tip-offs are:

You sink into carpeting *and* linoleum.

You need more than one umbrella.

After you get out of the car, you have a steering wheel imprint on your stomach.

If you see warning signs like these, you'll need help controlling your intake of calories. However, try to avoid boring diets that allow only one source of food. Some people say that Jimmy Cagney *really* mashed a grapefruit in Mae Clark's face because she handed it to him just after he had finished a six-week grapefruit diet.

Suggestions like these can help you shed a few pounds:

When making a malt, leave the top off the blender.

Eat ice cream with a fork in front of the fireplace.

Slip-cover the freezer.

Store food up high—in the attic, for instance.

Sometimes getting up for a snack isn't worth the effort.

Throw out every sweet in the house—even the candy pills in the toy doctor kit.

Train your family to block your view of food commercials.

When you sit down, hold a child or pet on your lap. You'll have a harder time getting up for snacks.

To avoid making trips to the refrigerator while watching TV, tie your shoelaces together.

Wear a sleeveless dress when you go food shopping. You'll walk through the ice cream section faster.

Buy your ice cream cones in stores with long lines. There is a remote chance you might get tired of waiting.

Grocery shop with a friend. Give her your list and take hers so you won't throw extra goodies into the cart.

Your battle against calories is made more difficult by advertisers who do a superb job of making food seem irresistible. If you read magazines, newspapers, or watch TV, keeping your weight down is a serious challenge. By using your imagination, however, you can control your enthusiasm for food:

Pretend the frosting flowers on a cake have bees in them.

At mealtime, pretend you are at a cocktail party and eat your food on a tiny plate standing up.

Tell yourself that jumbo fried shrimp are out of season.

It is a well-known fact that extra calories can be eliminated by physical activity, so supplement your diet with a plan of exercise. Here are a few suggestions:

Don't use the garage door opener. Better yet, don't use the garage. In the winter you'll get exercise scraping ice off your car windows.

Eat in cafeterias rather than restaurants. You'll burn off a few calories walking through the line.

Root for both teams at sporting events. You'll shed more pounds jumping up to cheer for both sides.

For years, football players have known the value of cheerleaders. Why not cheer yourself on with inspiring mottos so you can stick to your weight reduction program? Here are a few:

To Reduce, Don't Eat the Mousse.

Bending and Stretching Will Make You Look Fetching.

Bakery Bags Make Saddle Bags.

Pieces of Pie Stay on the Thigh.

A Bonbon is Never Gone.

Don't Dillydally at the Deli.

Remember, you are on your own and your fight is a hard one. Friends invite you to eat calorie-laden food, advertisers give lavish descriptions of their food products, and restaurants do not have dessert and non-dessert sections.

Of course, you can become overly zealous in your drive to lose weight. You'll know you've over-dieted if someone asks you to lay your body on a package so she can tie a knot, or if you wear a flowered hat and somebody tries to pick you.

Chapter 5

Did Jackie Kennedy Make up Casseroles When She Took Her Job at Doubleday?

Cancel your subscriptions
When you join the working force;
Stay away from bookstores—
Or else take a speed-reading course.

Getting friendly with potential baby-sitters and freezing fifty pounds of lunch meat are two things you will naturally do when you start working. But if you put your mind to it, you can find other ways to prepare yourself and your family for your new way of life. For instance, you can add to your list of frequently-called numbers the phone number of a pizza parlor that delivers.

Here are some other preparations you can make:

Write next year's Christmas and birthday cards. You might also want to address a get-well card to an accident-prone friend.

Pick a fight with your coffee-klatch and lunch friends so you won't feel sad that you can't join them.

Call your mother and mother-in-law often and at inconvenient times so they would rather not hear from you.

Buy an alarm clock. You can't rely on your baby to wake you up.

Buy a briefcase. Don't try to get by with an old diaper bag.

Start packing your family's lunches with stale bread and overripe bananas so they will want to pack their own.

Buy some large laundry baskets. Dirty laundry will accumulate.

Try on the fifty pairs of panty hose in your drawer to see which are wearable. Force yourself to throw out the others.

Before you take a deal on 1,000 lunch bags, find out whether the gang eats in or goes out for lunch.

If you are hooked on Johnny Carson or David Letterman, buy a VCR so you can watch them while chopping vegetables for supper.

Practice driving in rush-hour traffic.

Don't think that your children will become your little assistants when you start working. They won't. In fact, they might even try to sabotage your efforts. Therefore, make some special preparations:

Join your children and their friends at play so they will get sick of you and be happy you found a job.

Buy some strong glue. More things will get broken when you're not around to supervise.

Give your kids a crash course in table manners. No longer will they be eating only in front of you.

If your child sucks his thumb, break him of the habit. People will think you made him insecure by going to work.

Forbid your daughter to have boys in while you work. Tell her to have them stand by the birdfeeder and that she can watch them through the window.

Go to PTA meetings and ask questions so people will notice you are attending in case you can't get there after you start working.

Join your children at play so they'll get sick of you.

Practice walking backwards so you can do it success-fully when you leave your child with a sitter.

Try especially hard to anticipate problems and stay on top of your situation. For example, draw up a list of friends your children can't have over when you're not around. How-ever, you needn't go so far as one single mother who ran an ad to meet a man whose mother would baby-sit.

Chapter 6

Stapling a Falling Hem Is Tacky

Take more time to pluck your brows;
Go slower now and slave o'er it
If someone looks and says to you
"The left one is my favorite."

Since clothes and grooming affect your success at work, try hard to look like a "do" instead of a "don't" picture. At the same time, don't be overly solicitous about your appearance, like the woman who always put on new makeup and changed into another outfit for the coffee break.

At the very least, pay enough attention to how you look to insure that you don't get fired. Whether you like it or not, people judge you by how you dress. If you're savvy, you'll know how to use that to your advantage. Remember: dressing well can make you appear more competent than you really are.

Here are a few tips that will lead to a more capable, desirable look:

Unless it looks like a mole, remove the speck that gets between your leg and your panty hose.

If you have a run in your panty hose, wear them so the run comes on the inside of the leg. Then put a note where you'll see it, saying DON'T CROSS YOUR LEGS.

If you wear a V-neck to work, be sure it's a small *v* instead of a capital V.

17

Don't wear your collar up unless you want to spend a lot of time saying "I *want* it up" to people who try to turn it down.

If people sneeze often in your presence, check your clothes for dog or cat hair.

Don't buy gloves; they're no longer necessary (unless you're a surgeon or a surgical nurse).

Check your mascara often. Mascara is like Ted Kennedy—you don't know just when, but you're sure it's going to run.

If people keep saying "You don't look well" and you feel just fine, have your colors done.

Check your clothes more carefully if you hear "What happened to *you*?" more than five times a week.

A dowdy appearance not only makes you seem less together but actually distracts your co-workers. In order not to waste other people's time, follow these grooming tips:

If people sneeze often in your presence, check your clothes for dog or cat hair.

Don't put makeup over the sleep crust in your eyes.

Don't buy anything that's supposed to look good wrinkled. You'll only have to explain that to people.

Don't ask, "Who can tie a bow?" every time you wear a bow. Get up an hour earlier.

Don't try to get out a smudge of dirt on your white skirt by applying White-Out.

Don't pierce more than one hole in each ear. It takes too long to find two pairs of earrings to match your outfit.

Don't throw all your necklaces and chains together in your jewelry box. You can't be sure you'll hit enough red lights on the way to work to get them untangled.

Don't buy lipstick on sale. The only shades ever marked down are walnut and evergreen.

Don't buy a monogrammed item that doesn't have *your* initial on it even if it's on sale.

Don't have candy-cane teeth. Check them for lipstick stains.

Don't wear shoulder pads so big they overlap your padded bra.

Don't wear so much makeup your child can finger-paint from your face.

You might feel frustrated with the sheer number of choices you must make about clothes and grooming. You may not even know whether or not you have good taste. You'll know you don't if the dress you're thinking about buying is *always* there when you go back to look at it.

Chapter 7

Don't Draw Funny Pictures of Your Boss on the Computer

Two people give you orders
And are breathing down your neck;
The one you'd better favor
Is the one who signs your check.

Doing well at work requires more than simple competence. You must create an impression of excellence in other people's minds. For example, if you have a tendency to make errors, pretend you're energy-conscious and work in dim light. Your mistakes will be less noticeable.

Here are a few more tips for making a positive impression:

If someone asks you for the time, don't give it immediately as if you've been watching the clock.

If everyone chips in for a gift for someone, sign your name at the very bottom of the card, even though you might have been approached first. People will think the collection was your idea.

Don't say "Excuse me" after every yawn. You'll only draw attention to them.

Tell people you're on medication. Although it's only the pill, people will be nicer to you.

Try to separate working and parenting. For instance, if you're at a board meeting and the president says "On July 31 we are going to merge with Apex Instruments," don't say "July 31? Why, that's Jennifer's birthday!"

Of course, to be successful you must get on the boss's good side. Unfortunately, this isn't something you can do by 10:00 A.M. and then go on to other things. Convincing him or her that you are a very valuable employee is a full-time job. To be successful, follow these tips:

Get to know the office cleaning staff and mention them to your boss. It will seem as if you're putting in a lot of overtime.

Don't make the boss feel like a bully. If he calls you into his office to reprimand you, don't carry along a box of tissues.

Frequently ask him to retell a joke.

If she catches you photocopying a recipe, tell her you're planning a surprise party for her and you're preparing the menu.

If you have your children's picture on your desk, be sure it shows them playing with his children at the office picnic.

If she wants to look through your wastebasket, don't ask her if she's got a search warrant.

Learn the Heimlich maneuver and invite him over for a dinner of bony fish. You may get to save his life.

Your boss will like you more if you seem steady and dependable, so try not to stay out sick. However, if you must be away from work, prepare people for your absence. The day before you plan to stay home, try ideas like these:

Ask around the office to see if anyone has an antihistamine.

When you put down your coffee cup, say "Make sure no one drinks from this."

Wear a color that makes you look pale.

Some women don't want to work their way up the ladder.

Several times, drop what you're doing and rush to the rest room.

Do your best every day and remember to create a competent, "power" image. Get to work on time and *don't* have a license plate that reads TGIF. And if you're trying to work your way up to manager, don't let anyone overhear you argue with your kids over the telephone; they'll lose respect for your managerial skills.

Chapter 8

I'm Late for Work— You'll Have to Go with One Shoe

One night you forget
To pull the clock stem,
Next morning you need
A stitch in your hem.

Getting to work on time is a job in itself. Morning is rush time—that's *Rush* with a capital R. One woman, for example, was running late and got arrested for speeding on the way to work. As the policeman was writing the ticket, she used his badge as a mirror to put on her makeup.

Doing yoga or chanting a mantra is out of the question, so you'll have to find a different method of relieving the pressure. Be organized. You don't have to turn your home into boot camp, but you can try suggestions like these:

Don't risk losing your car keys. Either sleep with them around your neck or have five duplicate sets made.

File your fingernails before you go to bed so you won't put a run in your panty hose.

Set your alarm. The telephone time lady won't give you a wake-up call.

Morning problems are often child-related. For instance,

you're helpless at breakfast because you can't say "Eat or you won't get dessert!" If you're having trouble dealing with your children in the morning, try tactics like these:

Start waking your children early, but not before 4:00 A.M.

As each kid gets ready, plunk him in the car and belt him in.

If you're in such a hurry that you have to scribble your child's sickness excuse, write M.D. after your name. You could also have a rubber stamp made of your signature.

If you're out of milk, don't think your children will eat their cereal dry. They won't. Get some ice cream out of the freezer and let it melt.

Here's one corner you might regret cutting.

If your kids ask you to drill them on their spelling words, just keep working and ask them how to spell words like *toaster, cereal,* and *cocoa.*

Learn how to organize search parties for missing shoes.

Hide the toy from the cereal box so your child doesn't waste time playing with it.

Use a home computer to get the right kid to the right sitter and the right school.

Drive a crummy-looking car. You can leave later because your kids will want to be dropped off a few blocks from school.

Streamline your morning routine, but don't cut too many corners. For example, *never* send anyone under twelve out to warm up the car.

Chapter 9

Don't Call Mommy at Work Today, Unless the Sitter Runs Away

*Don't hesitate to tell your kids
"Don't call me—I'll call you."
Far meaner folks will say these words
To them their whole life through.*

Do you cringe when your child calls you at work? Many mothers do. In fact, children's calls can be so disruptive that certain employers will only hire sterilized grandmothers.

Teach your children to distinguish between emergency and non-emergency calls. For instance, when a child gets the smaller "half" of a candy bar it's not an emergency; when a child *steals* a candy bar, it is.

As every working mother knows, however, children have a low emergency threshold. The variety of their calls is endless. The most common one is the tattletale call, when you have to say "Put Kevin on." Here are some actual calls to mothers at work:

"There's nothing good on TV."

"My foot's asleep."

"Mark told me to shut up."

26

Teach your children the difference between emergency and non-emergency calls.

"Allison colored in my coloring book."

"We're out of toilet paper."

"Can I sit by the car window the next time we go to Grandma's?"

Some calls do more than make you cringe. They make you wonder if working is worth the effort. Calls like these can make you break out in hives:

"Our baby-sitter told us we were so good we can sit for ourselves the rest of the day."

"Snoopy forgot to scratch at the door when he was supposed to."

"We just had a door-to-door rummage sale with stuff from the attic."

"You said you wanted the living room painted, so we found some old paint in the basement and did it."

"Jessica crossed the street and made a car screech its brakes."

You can't prevent your child from calling you at work, but you might be able to develop a sixth sense for when he or she will call. One mother said, "I can tell when it's going to be Bobby—his calls have a whiny ring."

Repeated calls can be quite trying, so remember to keep calm. Here are some things you can do to handle children's calls:

Don't answer with a crabby "Now what?" When you hang up, you'll feel guilty and won't be able to concentrate on your work.

Don't say "Operator, please trace this call and have the caller arrested."

Tell them their grandma is lonesome and they should call *her.*

Say "I'm glad you called because there's something I want to add to your chore list."

Don't say to your boss "You should just be thankful *you* don't have to solve the problem."

Don't say to the boss "Quit tapping your watch—it makes me nervous!"

Getting calls at work is frustrating, but your situation could be worse—your children could have called you while you were being interviewed. You do have things to be grateful for. At least you know that, while they're on the phone to you, your kids aren't playing in traffic, hitting their sisters and brothers, or eating what you fixed for supper.

Chapter 10

Put Him on the Phone—I'll Talk Him down from on Top of the Cupboard

How to discipline the kids?
Your dear old grandma knew:
Tell them just the opposite
Of what you hope they'll do.

Since you have less time to discipline your children, you must learn to do it effectively. You have to get across to your children that what you tell them is important and they must remember it. For example, by age five, your child should know her name and address in case she gets lost. You can't stamp it on her forehead and expect a person to drop her in a mailbox.

Strive to find reprimands that work. You don't want to be just a droning sound in your children's ears. Here are some ideas for successful discipline:

Take notes at the staff meeting and repeat to your kids what the boss yelled at you.

When your child calls you at work, threaten to put your boss on the line. The way you've talked about your boss will make this sound scary.

Practice reprimanding your children by yelling at rotten drivers on the way home from work.

29

Write OR ELSE on the bottom of the chore list.

Tell your kids that the house is bugged.

Have as many extension phones as you have children. Then you can discipline them from work and only have to give the lecture once.

Be careful not to give punishments that will result in your own misery. Only a masochist would ground her children or forbid them to watch TV. Here are some other disciplinary measures a working mother should *not* take:

Don't say "Wait until your father gets home!" The sitter has probably been saying all day "Wait until your mother gets home!"

Don't call on your union steward to mediate a fight between your children at home.

Don't have them reenact the fight when you get home so you can decide who is guilty.

Don't promise them half your paycheck if they behave for the sitter.

Don't serve them breakfast in bed to avoid fights at the breakfast table.

Don't say to a co-worker "I'll handle your kids' calls if you'll take mine and discipline my children."

The bad news about being a mother today is that there are so many new ways to mess up your children. The good news is that there are so many problem kids, your failures will not be as noticeable.

Chapter 11

Make a Pothole Seem Like an Amusement Park

You'll have quality time
With a capital Q
When you say to your child
"I'm here only for you."

Working mothers relieve some of their guilt by spending "quality time" with their children. But what is quality time? It would be nice if a light went on to show you, but that doesn't happen. Sometimes it's easier to know what's not quality time, such as listening to your child while you're vacuuming.

Quality time means making the most of every experience you share with your children, such as letting them spray the stains while you do the laundry. If you're a busy working mother, you may find ideas like these helpful:

Occasionally get down on all fours—and not just to look for a shoe.

Take the phone off the hook when you're playing cards with your child.

If you read the newspaper while holding him, put him between you and the newspaper—not in back of it.

Use fresh water to get smudges off her face. Don't spit on your finger.

Quality time.   *Non-quality time.*

Get her name right. Don't continually call her by her sister's name. Calling her "Honey" or "Darling" will eliminate this danger.

If you take her someplace in a cab, make sure the cabdriver is pleasant. If he isn't, get out immediately.

Lift the child up to push the elevator button so he feels he's part of the adventure.

Let your child help navigate while you drive instead of just telling him to get his head out of the way so you can see the signs.

Always answer questions—even if you have to call the library.

Some mothers go overboard trying to provide quality time. If you find yourself dressing your daughter in jodhpurs just to take her on the merry-go-round, you're probably over-doing it. Watch for other signs of overkill:

Serving her Kool-Aid in your crystal stemware.

Putting on hand cream before you take her hand.

Playing classical music while you are talking to him—even while you are bawling him out.

Wiping his nose with a linen handkerchief.

Clipping a microphone on her sunsuit so you can hear what she says in the sandbox while you work in the kitchen.

Writing all notes to teachers and sitters on embossed stationery.

You're probably not in much danger of overdoing it, however. In fact, some days it's hard to squeeze in even ten seconds of quality time. This can be stressful, so focus on the rewards—like imagining your child valedictorian of the class because you always included her in discussions, even when she was in a high chair.

Chapter 12

Wild Bosses Couldn't Keep Me Away

You'll see the working mothers—
The back row is their fate.
They'll have to pull out early
Or else they've come in late.

Working mothers often feel guilty when they can't attend their children's programs, games, or school functions. They've watched too many movies in which a child suddenly sees Mom or Dad did get there after all and then sings beautifully or wins the game.

Getting to your child's program is not easy when you're trying to hold down a full-time job. Your boss might not let you go even if you promise not to take any coffee breaks or trips to the ladies' room for the rest of the week, so you may have to talk your way into it. Here are a few persuasive arguments:

"I'll do paperwork in the car during intermission."

"The company car in the school parking lot would be good advertising."

"I'll give out our firm's card to every parent and teacher there."

"If you don't let me go, you'll have to give me a raise to pay for the counseling my child will need because I didn't show up."

When your child has a part in a school play, just sending a telegram saying "Break a leg!" will not suffice. You'll have to show up—and stay long enough to be seen. Here is some more advice about school functions:

If your boss thinks your child won't know if you're in the audience, say you have a distinctive way of applauding that your child recognizes.

No matter how difficult it was to get time off to attend a game, don't bawl out the coach for not letting your child play more.

Instead of telling your son you had to get back to work, tell him the game got too exciting for you.

Don't yell "Boo!" at a concert just so there won't be an encore.

If you will have to leave the school building early, leave your car lights on. Someone will make an announcement and people will think that's why you walked out.

If you sneaked off without telling your boss, don't bring back a program. You may inadvertently start fanning yourself with it.

If you can't get there, have a friend sit in the back row wearing one of your dresses.

No matter how much pressure you're under, avoid shortcuts. For example, don't ask your child's teacher to hold a parent-teacher conference during your child's play. And don't ask anyone under three feet tall for directions out of the building; you might get back to work after closing hours.

Chapter 13

Tell Her She Can Write a "Kiddies Dearest" Book Someday

She comes to your house
And keeps your kids quiet.
But you're better off
If she's on a diet.

When your kids aren't at school, they're home with your most important ally: the baby-sitter. This woman's services are indispensable, so stay on her good side. The only thing worse than having your children cry when you leave for work is having the sitter cry too.

Having children that are acceptable to a sitter is vital. Note the word *acceptable*. The most you can hope for is that your sitter will have more good days with your children than bad days.

Here are a few tips to help you obtain—and keep—a sitter:

Have a substitute sitter. Don't expect your parents to fly standby from Akron when your sitter is sick.

Have a substitute sitter for your substitute sitter. If possible, have a substitute for your substitute for your substitute.

38

Even if you have an orange grove or an apple orchard in your backyard, leave food for your sitter.

Don't pay a sitter what you got when you did her job. If you do, she won't come next time you call.

Don't leave your children with a sitter who lives close to where you work. She can come and get you—or bring them to you.

Remember: two ten-year-old sitters are not equivalent to a twenty-year-old sitter.

Never tell your sitter that the TV is broken until you're ready to leave. Even then, she may beat you out the door.

When you get a raise, try not to act so happy that you give away the news. Your sitter will expect one too.

Telling your sitter "This is the number at which I can

Make sure to give your sitter a place to take cover.

be *bothered*" may discourage her from calling you unnecessarily.

Suggest that she put on makeup and comb her hair shortly before you get home so she won't look harrassed.

If your children are hellions, pull the sofa away from the wall so the sitter can take cover if necessary.

Sitters are like gas stations—some provide full service; some, mini service; and some, no service. Be vigilant! Don't be so eager to get a sitter that you hire a poor one. Keep these points in mind while evaluating people:

If you have to pay bail for your sitter before she can come, think about getting someone else.

Be suspicious if she is wearing sexy-smelling perfume. She didn't put it on for your kids.

She might be too young if she scribbles outside the lines when she is coloring with your children.

If she hands you a business card, her fee will be too high.

Like the woman who discovered that her children's babysitter kept earplugs in her ears, most mothers have had at least a few unhappy experiences with sitters. Here are some of their complaints:

"My two-year-old had to use the toilet and she said he was just doing isometrics."

"She was always on the phone. She wouldn't know it was raining outside unless the phone leaked."

"She'd make snacks—like pizza—but she'd burn them, and the smoke alarm would wake up the kids."

Not all sitters are bad news, though. That's a good thing, because working mothers need them so much they're likely to ignore warning signs. From time to time, however, things go seriously wrong. If you see signals like these you should say "I'm in trouble":

You come home and find the sitter's mother there.

Your sitter gets an unlisted number and won't give it to you.

When you call her to see if she's available, the sitter suddenly starts coughing as though she has a cold.

Most of the time, however, things work out all right. In fact, having a baby-sitter is a wonderful arrangement. You get paid more money than your sitter and she does the harder job. You might be tempted to take advantage of her, but don't. For instance, don't make her come over and put your kids to sleep. And don't hand her a video camera and ask her to capture all your child's "firsts." Ask for only three or four.

Chapter 14

God Bless the Sandman

Your kids are cute in PJ's
Hugging their Teddys,
But good luck trying to get them
Into their beddys.

Getting children to bed has always been a major challenge for a working mother, who needs her own sleep desperately. No one has invented a foolproof technique for inducing sleep, however, so you'll have to be crafty. Find out, for instance, what color walls make a child the drowsiest and which stories make a child fall asleep before the end. Perhaps you can find a fabric softener that makes sheets really relaxing, or take a course in hypnotism.

The great sense of relief you feel when your children finally fall asleep makes slumber a goal worth achieving. No child in history has ever admitted to being tired, so you can expect a rough time leading up to "Good-night." If you follow these tips, however, the process might go a little more smoothly:

Help your child with her homework. If it's beyond you, ask her for the phone number of the smartest kid she knows.

Make bedtime stories shorter. For example, in "Goldilocks" have Mama Bear be a single parent.

If your children get upset by any change in a story, don't leave anything out—just talk faster.

42

Show your children your boss's picture taken with a very severe look and say "If Mommy doesn't get to sleep on time tonight, this person will be mean to her in the morning."

Instead of telling your children a bedtime story, practice a presentation you have to make at work. They'll nod off in no time.

Getting your children to sleep can drive you to the brink of desperation. If you find yourself at your wits' end, try some of these suggestions:

Skip their baths so their bodies stick to the sheets.

If they yell "I didn't brush my teeth," tell them to use their fingers.

Teach the dog to growl every time they try to get out of bed.

Use sawhorses to keep traffic away from your street.

Play "Taps" for them.

Say "First one to sleep gets a Porsche when he's sixteen."

You can't have your kids arrested for loitering if they don't go to bed, so good luck finding creative ways to solve the problem. Even when you succeed, there's the little matter of getting them to stay in bed. The only thing you can do to insure *that* is to quickly tar the floor.

Chapter 15

You Can't Call in Sick with the Guilties

My work isn't hurting my children, I know;
"The guilties" have finally flown.
But one thing can make them return in a flash—
Kissing kids' owies by phone.

Day or night, you've got to provide for your children's needs, and you're likely to feel guilty about being away from home so much of the time. Don't berate yourself, however, because you're earning money, which benefits the entire family. In fact, your children should thank you. But even if they did, you'd probably still spend a lot of time wondering if you're a good mother.

Almost anything can make you feel guilty. For example, one mother lamented the fact that someone else had to tell her daughter there was no Santa Claus. She said, "If I had been around all the time I would have noticed she was becoming suspicious." Another woman was so worried about neglecting her child that she checked his stuffed animals for stiff fur to see if he had cried himself to sleep.

Asked to name times when they felt guilt pangs, some mothers said:

"When the phone book automatically opens to pizza parlors."

"When the applause at the end of my child's school production wakes me up."

45

"When I say 'Just *blow* Mommy a kiss because she's wearing her makeup.' "

"When I want to give my son a surprise birthday party and the only kid I know he plays with that I can invite is his brother."

"When the pictures from last year's birthday party are still in the camera."

"When I ask my co-workers to buy what my daughter is selling."

"When I don't ask my co-workers to buy what my daughter is selling."

"When I say 'You're so clean you don't need a bath tonight' and I'm lying."

A certain amount of guilt is natural, but many women make themselves miserable with ridiculous worries. One mother, for instance, tortured herself with the question "Will he date older women to get a mother figure?" She was apt to call co-workers by her child's name because she spent so much time worrying about him.

Don't waste energy worrying about whether or not you're a good mother. Instead, do positive things that will make you the best mother you can be—or at least appear that way. For example:

Always buy products that say "Tastes homemade."

Try to be present when stitches are either put in or taken out.

Try to have more events marked on your calendar that are child-related than work-related.

Buy your kids clothes with labels on the outside or with alligators on them so people know you're not spending all your money on yourself.

When you serve fast food, pass the salt and pepper.

Look in the thesaurus for alternative words for *hurry* so you aren't constantly saying "Hurry up" in the morning.

Say prayers with your children instead of having them call "Dial-a-prayer."

Guilt is such a distressing emotion that some working mothers resort to dishonorable means to avoid feeling it, such as taking a thermometer out of a child's mouth almost immediately so they won't see it rise above normal.

Chapter 16

Park Pavilions Don't Have Video Games

If your children misbehave
Despite how much you chide,
Run and find a picnic table
Under which to hide.

If you're not feeling guilty about your children, you're often feeling embarrassed by them—especially in front of your boss and co-workers. The most likely place for these people to meet your children (besides the telephone) is the annual company picnic. Most workplaces have one. Its object is to remove you from daily pressures so that when you get back to work you will function better. Since the picnic invitation always includes children, you can't come alone.

Ordinarily, your employer and co-workers do not see you with your children, so you might feel just a teensy bit nervous about the impression your kids will make. Here are a few tips for minimizing the damage your kids can do:

Be careful where you park your car. You don't want your kids to dent your boss's car while getting out of yours.

Try to get a picture of your boss's children ahead of time so your children will know whom not to hit.

If a child is ornery, tell everyone it's his nap time.

Fill your children's plates for them. They're apt to say "Yuck" if you let them choose from the food other people brought.

Starve your children the day before the picnic so they'll eat everything they're offered.

Take along a nice neighbor child so you'll have one well-behaved kid with you.

Have your children sit away from everyone else so others can't observe their table manners.

If you know your able-bodied teenage son won't be willing to help move picnic tables, have him come with his arm in a sling.

Worrying about the impression your kids create is nerve-wracking enough. You also have the problem of wanting to appear to be a perfect mother. Here are some ways to make people think you're competent:

Bring along a nice neighbor child so you'll have one well-behaved kid with you.

Arrive late so everyone will see your kids while they're clean.

Take the rubber floor mat from your car and put it on the bottom of the wading pool so the kids won't slip and hurt themselves.

Make sure the plates you give your children to eat from aren't the same ones they used to play frisbee.

Look into the cooler and say, in concerned tones, "Isn't there any milk?"

Your boss is proud to give a company picnic, so if you don't want to attend you'll need a creative excuse. Even then, you might meet resistance. So if you're going to excuse yourself by saying you're in labor, don't say the pains are more than ten minutes apart or you'll be expected to show up.

Chapter 17

Vending Machines Don't Have Dill Pickles

Please excuse my errors.
You've got to help me out.
I can't get near my work now—
My stomach's sticking out!

Working while pregnant can be trying. Employers, for instance, often selfishly insist that you work your normal hours. When one mother-to-be asked for time off to see the doctor to find out if she was having twins, her boss asked "Don't they have home ultrasound kits?" Co-workers can also be insensitive. They will do things like bring in catalogs with pictures of slender young women in bikinis or check the capacity sign in the elevator as you enter.

Perhaps you should receive benefits besides maternity leave. For example, you ought to be able to change desks so you aren't seated next to a Skinny-Minnie. And if your ankles swell, you should be allowed to wear your furry bunny slippers to work.

Whether or not you receive extra pregnancy benefits, do your best to separate work and baby. For instance, don't try to put your hands over the baby's ears whenever you hear an off-color joke. And don't say to your boss "The baby gets upset when you yell at me."

Because pregnancy places extra demands on working relationships, try especially hard to get along with your boss and co-workers. These suggestions might help make life at the office more satisfying:

Announce over the intercom that you are going to have a baby so people won't get mad because you told others before them.

Bring fattening treats frequently so co-workers won't be so svelte.

Find out when your boss's birthday is. If it's anywhere near your baby's due date, say that's when the baby is expected. Even if your baby isn't born on that day, your boss will feel flattered.

Since everyone watches what you eat, have an orange peel on your desk while you sneak junk food.

It's important to maintain a healthy image, since everyone will be watching what you eat.

Make your co-workers feel part of your pregnancy: set up a betting pool on whether you'll have a boy or a girl.

Avoid clock-watching. Nervous co-workers will think you're timing labor pains.

Other people will make allowances for you, so return the favor. For example, don't get upset when male co-workers make hackneyed jokes like "You must have swallowed a watermelon seed." Tell yourself that someday doctors will find a way for men to have babies and you can make jokes about footballs. And don't ask people to look at your eyes rather than your stomach while you speak to them; at least they're not noticing how tired you look. Here are some other no-no's for the working mother-to-be:

Don't take a longer lunch hour just because you're eating for two.

No matter how thrilled you are about being pregnant, don't ask co-workers to feel the baby kick. If you absolutely must ask someone, make sure the person works in your department.

Don't hum lullabies to remind people you're pregnant.

Don't talk about childbirth with mothers who use words that are stronger than *discomfort* to describe pain.

Try not to talk co-workers into having children just so you can discuss babies during your coffee break.

Don't tell them whether or not you're going to breast-feed. Whatever you've decided, you're bound to start a controversy.

Don't choose co-workers as godparents. Someone will be jealous.

Working while pregnant does have a few fringe benefits. When you're on your way to the restroom, for example, people won't stop you and ask you to do something for them. You can use the breathing techniques you're learning in your Lamaze class to help reduce stress. And you'll be sober at the

Christmas office party, which will be a good time to get something on co-workers who've had a few too many.

Working while pregnant doesn't have to be overwhelming for you, your co-workers, or your employer. In fact, you can point out to your boss that you're a much better employee: you have such a hard time getting out of your chair, you spend more time at your desk.

Chapter 18

Where Can You Get a Male Chauvinist Deprogrammed?

He thinks a woman's business card
Is something he can disregard.
He thinks she shouldn't be so bold
But only do what she is told.

Even though many male employers are enlightened, from time to time you will come across one who makes Archie Bunker look like Alan Alda. The feminist movement hasn't raised this man's consciousness—only his blood pressure. His attitude is, If I can't say anything demeaning about a woman, I won't say anything.

You will recognize this type of man by his bizarre behavior:

When he uses abbreviations like GNP, he tells women what they stand for.

The only time he compliments a woman on an accomplishment is when she brings in something she baked for the coffee break.

Any time a woman calls in sick, he's convinced it's due to her period.

Whenever he sees Ms., he crowds in an *i* and another *s*, or an *r*.

55

Some bosses can make Archie Bunker look like Alan Alda.

When he is working a crossword puzzle, he only asks women for help with words that have to do with cooking or sewing.

He thinks women's initials belong only at the bottom of a letter and not on an attaché case.

The only time he ever comes close to talking about his feelings is when he pinches his finger in a desk drawer.

He refuses to go to the wedding of any woman who is going to keep her own name.

He expects women who work for him to worship the ground he walks on—and vacuum it, too.

You will know that your boss is suffering from an extreme case of male chauvinism if you see a Gloria Steinem dart board on his wall or if he gives men time off for voting and not women. You might also see signs that his wife is not liberated. For example, he may get away with asking "Where were you?" when she doesn't answer the phone on the first or second ring.

Men who do not believe in equality of the sexes inevitably make statements that anger you. Then, with the most innocent expression, they will ask "What did I say?" Here are some typical chauvinistic statements:

"Now do you have any questions—like, 'Am I allowed to knit during board meetings?' "

"Why don't you have yourself a good little cry?"

"Some of my best friends are women. In fact, my mother was a woman."

"I'm sorry we don't have any of your magazines in the employee lounge—just *Business Week* and *Sports Illustrated*."

"A company runs better when men are in charge."

"You should be home gathering material to put in your kid's baby book."

"Sew on this button for me, will you?"

What can be done about a man who makes statements like these? Unfortunately, not much. Many working women have tried unsuccessfully to enlighten a confirmed chauvinist. Here are some ideas worth trying:

Hang a picture of Archie Bunker with a red diagonal line through it.

Sarcastically say "This *is* the twentieth century, isn't it?"

Make a scrapbook of women achievers and give it to him.

Even if a confirmed chauvinist does come around, he's likely to keep his conversion a secret. Unfortunately, that means you'll never really know if he's enlightened or not, so you'll have to protect yourself with statements like "I worked on a report last night." Just don't let him know it was your son's book report.

Chapter 19

She Even Put Meringue on Her Mud Pies

Mrs. Perfect comes home
To a crock pot roast,
But when I arrive home
All I smell is burnt toast.

Another person who will plague you is a Mrs. Perfect. This woman makes you feel inferior. She doesn't set out to do this; it just happens.

Her standards are so high you need a telescope to see them. You're certain she sings a duet in the morning with the singer on her radio alarm. You'd like to report her to someone, but she never does anything wrong.

A Mrs. Perfect at work is even more irritating than one at home because you know she is juggling husband, house, work, kids, civic duties, and social life, yet every move she makes has a wonderful result.

How can you recognize a Mrs. Perfect? The clues are unmistakable:

The references on her resumé are nationally-known people.

She always gets into the building before it starts to rain.

She never tells a joke anyone has heard before.

58

She is a "morning" and a "Monday" person.

Her penmanship is always the best of anyone signing a card or petition.

The only time she watches a clock is when she is on a break.

Her desk calendar always shows the correct date.

She selects the right key on her key ring first.

She is only called into the boss's office to be praised or given a raise.

Even more discouraging to mortals is the fact that Mrs. Perfect's looks are flawless. She never has spinach on her teeth, for example, or toilet paper stuck to her shoe. Looking at her is cause for despair:

Her ankles seem even shapelier at the end of the day.

She gets carbon on a white skirt and it looks like a design.

When asked how she got such a lovely complexion, she credits soap and water.

If everyone wears a uniform, it looks best on her.

Her hair looks professionally styled—even on a rainy day.

Her picture is always in the company newsletter.

The picture on her ID badge looks as if it was taken by a Hollywood photographer.

Is she the only perfect one? Of course not. Her children are even better—or should I say *worse*? They will carry empty trash cans back to the garage without being told to do so, and frequently call their mother at work to tell her they have finished the chore list and ask what else needs to be done. Here is further evidence of their discouraging behavior:

They always carry pocket dictionaries.

When they sit on Santa's lap, they ask for world peace.

They have been to the police department only on field trips.

Their show-and-tells at school get standing ovations.

They ask their mother to videotape the president's speeches when they aren't going to be home.

They start out telephone calls to their mother at work by telling whoever answers "Mommy says she loves working with you!"

Their bedrooms would pass army inspections.

They look like the kids on TV commercials.

The baby-sitter doesn't mind if their mother picks them up late.

When her son plays doctor, he's a psychiatrist.

Fortunately, Mrs. Perfect's children do not work with you. Most of the time, you only have to put up with her.

The most upsetting thing about a Mrs. Perfect is the consistency of her performance. *Always* and *never* can be used accurately to describe her. That's why she isn't really an inspiration. You can only be inspired by someone when you believe that you can be like her. And if a woman comes back to work *stuffed* by a bowl of bouillon, you know for sure you'll never measure up.

Chapter 20

Where Is Recess
Now That I Need It?

If stress at work
Is far from funny
It helps to think
"I'm here for the money."

Their harried lives make working mothers one of the high-est-risk groups for stress. Employed mothers have almost no relaxation time, since everywhere they look they see some work for which they are responsible. One woman, for example, was told she would feel more relaxed if she imagined her business associates in their underwear, but that only made her think of all the laundry that was piled up at home.

When you get a cold, you have clear-cut symptoms like sneezes and a runny nose. When you're stressed, however, your symptoms are more subtle, and often seem unconnected to the real problem. So the first step toward relieving stress is to be aware of how much pressure you're under. The next step is to watch for symptoms like these:

You push the elevator button more than five times.

You tap your foot when there's no music playing.

Your answer to "Have a nice day" is something like "Easy for *you* to say" or "I have *other* plans."

One major cause of stress is trying to get to the top of your profession. An effective antidote, therefore, is to pretend you're already there. Buy a sign to put on your desk that says

Make an excuse to go to another floor so you can listen to the elevator music.

THE BUCK STOPS HERE. You can also give someone else a hard time; it seems a lot of people try this.

Here are a few other ways to manage stress:

If you smoke, blow a smoke ring and imagine it around the neck of the person who upsets you the most.

Make an excuse to go to another floor so you can listen to the elevator music.

Pull weeds from the office planter.

Drink a lot of coffee so you can go to the rest room every hour.

Put the picture of your family face down. Looking at it might give you additional stressful thoughts.

Try to think of the positive side of everything that happens. For example, if you have to work overtime, tell yourself "I'll miss rush-hour traffic."

Do something physical during your lunch hour. For example, help smooth cement being poured at a nearby building.

Throw dishes. You'll have to wait until you get home to do this—the paper cups and plastic spoons in the office lunchroom won't satisfy your needs.

Knit or crochet during your break. If you don't do handicrafts, tie and untie your shoelaces.

Tell someone off, even if you have to call the telephone time lady and bawl her out for not answering sooner.

Don't read magazines that have pictures of beautiful homes. You'll feel stressed because your house looks so different.

Take deep breaths, but not so many that people will think you're having trouble breathing and call the paramedics.

Do not take stress lightly. In fact, if stress is a problem, you might even have to take a leave of absence to deal with it. Just don't do that during your probationary period.

Chapter 21

Do Working Mothers Really Sort Socks on Their Lunch Hours?

I was that blur
You saw this noon,
Running my errands—
Crazed like a loon.

You're free of work on your lunch hour, but that doesn't make the time any less stressful. When both hands are on the twelve, the pressure is on! You have a list of things to do during your lunch hour and you never get every task checked off. As one mother said, "I move so fast, I'm afraid I'll be accused of shoplifting."

Don't you wish you could reserve a parking stall from 12:00 to 1:00? And wouldn't you like to have teammates, like in a relay race? Somebody would be at the door of the dry cleaner to grab your clothes so you could rush on. Maybe stores should have an express checkout for working mothers on their lunch hours.

One way to beat the rush is to bring household chores with you to work. Try to be casual about it, however. Don't follow the example of one mother, who walked into the lunchroom with a travel iron and her daughter's wrinkled dress. She said to her co-workers, "You folks don't mind holding up your coffee cups while I press this, do you?"

Although you might be embarrassed to bring your housework to the office, you can find other ways to use your lunch hour effectively, such as these:

Keep your errands a secret, or you'll hear "While you're there, would you get me some . . . . "

Remember, every second counts. Instead of ordering a BLT, order a BL or a B.

If you meet an old friend, instead of standing and visiting with her ask her to run errands with you.

Bring your photo album to work with you and paste pictures in it during lunch. You can get the pictures in the book and show them off at the same time.

If you hear someone say "I'm bored," rip your errand list down the middle and give that person half.

Eat your sandwich while you're standing in line at the department store exchange counter. When you're done, you can blow up your sandwich bag and pop it to get the clerk's attention.

Learn your children's sizes so you don't have to look around and find a child as big as yours and ask his mother what size he wears.

Be prepared to adjust your lunch-hour plans. For example, if someone asks you in the morning for a ride home, you'll have to spend the time cleaning out your car.

As your lunch-hour list grows, remove items from your lunch bag that you know you won't have time to eat.

Find a job at the mall.

Take off your sweatband before you walk back into the office building.

You're likely to get in trouble if you come back late from lunch, so try not to cram in too many errands. Here are some other noon-hour no-no's:

If you stop in at a supermarket to buy your lunch, don't eat it on the way to the checkout—you could get arrested.

Don't finish typing your child's term paper on your lunch hour. The typeface on the $2,000 machine at work will never match the letters on your $100 typewriter at home.

If you get back late from lunch, don't defend yourself by saying "I was cashing my check." The boss might say "If it took the teller that long to count out your money, I'm paying you too much!"

From time to time, you can avoid all the fuss of running errands by going home on your lunch break. This has its benefits. After all, it's the only time you don't have to share the TV. Besides, you can get ahead on your housework. You can also brush the breakfast crumbs off the counter to make room for the supper crumbs.

Chapter 22

Don't Put Your Apron on over Your Coat

Take off your press-on nails,
Put on your heels so low,
Stuff earplugs in your ears,
Then go! go! go!

You race-walk to your car after work to face the worst hour of the day—the time between work and dinner. While you're laying rubber on the parking lot, you're trying to remember what you need to buy on the way home. You even find rush-hour traffic in the grocery store. Ten-items-or-less aisles are jammed this time of day.

You try to get home as quickly as you can because you never know what kind of crisis your kids are creating in your absence. You need a speedy commute, so try a few of these tactics:

Don't say "Good night" to your co-workers—just "'Night" will do.

Keep a sign handy to hold up in case your car breaks down: MY KIDS NEED ME AT HOME.

Don't look at the clock in your car. You'll drive too fast because you'll see how little time you have to fix dinner.

When you stop to pick up fast food, you'll feel like a better mother if you ask "Is that lettuce in the bun Romaine, Bibb, or Boston?"

Don't yell at the waitress at the fast-food counter "And make it snappy!"

Use your time at stoplights to open packages for dinner.

Don't listen to the news as you arrive home. Hearing about depressing situations and then walking in your door could be more than you can handle.

Of course, when you tear into your driveway, chances are there isn't room to park. You'll probably have to get out of the car to remove a tricycle or a doll buggy from your path. Although you've packed two lunchboxes for each child, they will all say "I'm hungry!" as you walk through the door. Even the dog is apt to come up to you with his dish in his mouth.

These things are trying but you can handle them with just a little patience. Others, however, require fortitude, such as:

You know you're in trouble when...

A child handing you a plunger.

A child saying "You've got a pillow feather in your hair."

A child licking the cookie jar so he can eat all the crumbs from the cookies you made three years ago.

Finding distressing situations at home is not the only difficulty you face at the end of a day. You're also likely to have a hard time switching hats from professional work to mothering. This isn't surprising, since each job requires different skills. Besides, you've gotten used to being thanked for what you do at work.

To survive that first hour at home, try some of these suggestions:

Don't even try for quality time.

Learn to mix with a beater and stir with a spoon at the same time.

Hold an ice pack to your head as you work around the kitchen. The children might feel sorry for you and help—or at least behave.

Get out your frustrations by grating cheese. (You can always use cheese on something.)

Think of a joke you heard at work today, but don't tell it to your children.

Chop an onion. Crying will make you feel better.

If you feel you must say "I'm beat!" say it to your dog or your reflection in the mirror. That way, you won't risk a mean answer.

To save time setting the table, tell your family to pretend they're at an airport and eat standing up.

If you have a female boss, console yourself with the thought that she's going through the same thing you are.

Make sure that stress does not impair your judgment. For instance, don't complain to City Hall that the traffic lights are set wrong because you didn't get all green ones on the way home. Don't provoke your children to misbehave just so you can send them to their rooms. Realize it won't help to promise your kids you'll tell them some good office gossip during dinner if they behave.

Probably the best way to survive the transition from work life to home life is to stretch your sense of time. For instance, imagine that each minute lasts an hour. Of course, you can go too far. You know you're in trouble when you have thirty seconds while the kids wash their hands for dinner and you think "What am I going to do with all this free time?"

Chapter 23

There Is Life after a Day's Work

Staying awake in the evening
Is tough but you just have to do it.
It's best to go to a movie—
Because you can sleep right through it.

You've heard of the game "Keep Away." Well, a much more challenging one is "Keep Awake"—the game you play every evening. After you rise early, dress, pack lunches, get kids organized, give them breakfast, get them to school or day care, and then work eight hours, *tired* doesn't adequately describe how you feel.

One employed mother said she didn't dare read a magazine while standing in the checkout aisle because after one paragraph she would fall asleep. Another working mother dozed while reading the list of ingredients on a box of cereal.

The moments after you arrive home are a perilous time. Whatever you do, don't sit down immediately. Here are a few tips to help you keep your eyelids open:

Pretend you see wet paint signs on all the furniture.

Immediately open the bills in your mail.

Don't run the dishwasher. The sound is lulling.

Play a John Philip Sousa record.

Tell yourself "If I take a nap now I'll be awake half the night."

Dust something. Sneezing wakes you up.

"Keep awake" is a game working mothers play every evening.

If you manage to stay awake, don't just sit around every evening. You don't want to turn into a couch potato, so force yourself to go out. Here are a few methods for staying awake through an evening out:

Don't put cream in your coffee, even if you ordinarily do. You want the full effect of the caffeine.

Call home. You will no doubt hear something to worry about that will take away your sleepiness.

Sit next to the biggest gossip. You'll stay awake so you won't miss anything.

Park far away from your destination. The fresh air will be invigorating. Run as much of the distance as possible without ruining your deodorant.

Even if the speaker was rotten, start a standing ovation.

Do some calisthenics in the bathroom, but be careful not to break anything.

If there is a raffle, buy a lot of tickets. You'll try hard to be awake for the drawing.

If you start to doze, pretend you lost a contact. While everyone is on hands and knees looking for it, you can catch a bit of shut-eye.

You can insure a social life by joining a group that meets regularly. Bridge clubs, for example, serve this purpose. Unfortunately, you can't always count on the excitement of the game to keep you awake. If you play bridge, try some of these suggestions to keep from falling asleep:

Wear fuchsia nail polish.

Put up the card tables carelessly. A collapsing table leg will wake you up quickly.

Offer to check on the hostess's sleeping children when you are dummy. You can catch forty winks there. (That's better than napping at the table.)

Shuffle the cards really fast so the gusts of air hit your face.

At a certain stage of sleepiness, staying awake is impossible. Keep a pair of sunglasses handy to conceal the fact that your lids are closed, or else announce to everybody "I'll be back in a minute" and unabashedly doze.

Chapter 24

It's Hard To Dazzle When You're Worn to a Frazzle

If you ask him how his day was,
Marriage will be sublimer.
But after you have asked him,
Don't quickly set the timer.

When you go back to work, you'll have to work hard at everything—especially at keeping your marriage happy. For example, if you wake up in a bad mood, try not to criticize your husband. Let someone he works with tell him his suit coat is buttoned wrong.

Sustaining the bliss of marriage is no picnic when you're working. You might need the help of experts, particularly ones who can help you maintain a healthy sex life. Keep their recommendations in mind:

Wear sexy sleepwear. Do not go from a gray flannel suit to a gray flannel nightgown. And don't let the only see-through item you wear to bed be a hairnet.

Write love notes with shocking suggestions and put them in with his lunch, but never write them on the back of your business cards.

Don't brush off his dandruff before you lay your head on his shoulder.

If you don't have any work that has to be done at

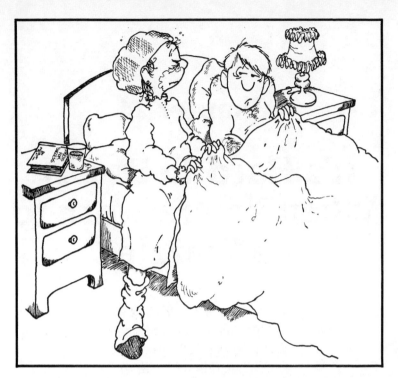

Don't let the only see-through item you wear to bed be a hairnet.

night, bring home a briefcase, throw it in a corner and say "I'm not going to waste my time on this when you're around."

If you *must* do some work, do it behind the cover of a sexy magazine.

Ask him to help you fold the clothes and be sure your best lacy unmentionables are among them.

Make sure your husband feels he is more important to you than the children. For example, never say "Not tonight, Honey—one of the kids has a headache."

Beyond sexuality, you'll have psychological issues to think about. Your husband might be bothered by things that wouldn't occur to you. Try to be aware of his fears. He might have felt humiliated when you entered the work force. Or he may feel like a latchkey husband. You can help restore his self-esteem by following some of these suggestions:

Buy a sleeper-beeper and wear it when you sit down with your husband after dinner.

Put his picture in your billfold ahead of your credit cards.

If you get an award from work, be sure to thank your husband when receiving it. Blow him a kiss, and wink.

If the award is a plaque, don't bother to dust it; he'll think it doesn't mean that much to you.

Fix items for dinner that don't take a lot of chewing, like soup, so you can talk more.

Join a health club together. Make sure he stands in the front row during aerobics so he doesn't compare other bodies with yours.

Put up some of his work on the refrigerator along with the kids' drawings.

After a quarrel, don't feel you have to get him to admit that you're right. Tell a friend about the fight and *she* will agree with you.

When he stops in at work to see you, hold his hand as you take him around to meet your co-workers.

Write his name in much larger letters than the other names on your calendar when you have a lunch date with him.

Stay together during grocery shopping. Don't rip the list in half.

If you get a call-waiting signal when talking to him, say "I wouldn't take that but it's probably the jeweler telling me your birthday present is in."

If he's late picking you up at work, don't scold him. Instead say "Absence makes the heart grow fonder—and so does tardiness."

There isn't anything mysterious about keeping romance in marriage. It's mostly common sense, like not eating garlic-flavored chips from the vending machine just before leaving the office.

Chapter 25

All's Fair in Love and Work

Does five minutes extra
When fixing up your hair
Make him feel sure that
You're having an affair?

If you have a jealous husband, you've got it rough. Try as you might, you can't convince him that you aren't interested in the mailroom clerk. Don't be surprised if he shows people your wedding album at office parties or slips garlic into your scrambled eggs.

You try desperately to keep him from thinking about the men you work with, but to no avail. You can't even get him to be happy about the good things that happen to you. For instance, if you get a promotion, he gets angry because he thinks you got it by being nice to the men above you at work.

Wives with jealous husbands often make complaints like these:

"He only lets me have pink thread in my office sewing kit so I won't sew on buttons for men."

"He won't let me go to work on nights when the moon is full."

"He sneaks my makeup case out of my purse."

"If I'm hoarse, he makes me stay home because he thinks my voice sounds sexy."

"He waters down my perfume."

Jealous husbands have been known to bring their wedding albums to office parties.

"He makes me take a thermos of water to work so I won't bend over at the drinking fountain."

"He encourages the kids to call me at work."

"He makes me stay home on the days my horoscope involves a man."

"He hides my lunch so he can bring it to me at work."

"When I broke my arm, he wouldn't let me go back to work until it was completely healed because he didn't want other men to help me."

"He loves rainy vacations. He hates to have me go back to work with a beautiful tan."

You can't end your husband's jealousy, so be patient and do small things to show him how much you love him:

Polish your wedding ring when you know he's watching.

If you have a man's business card in your wallet, write a grocery list on the back of it so it seems unimportant to you.

If a man is leaving work with you and you know your husband is waiting outside, stop in the rest room for a few minutes.

If you get a speeding ticket on the way to work, tell your husband you got it on your way home. He'll think you were hurrying home to him instead of rushing to work.

Don't tell an off-color joke. He'll never believe a woman told it to you.

Don't tell your husband you watched a film at work. He'll worry about who sat next to you in the dark.

Never ask him if your stockings have a run or if your slip is showing. You can't depend on him to tell you the truth.

Never answer your work phone while laughing. Your husband could be on the line.

Tell him the lounge is so smoky, you and your co-workers can barely see each other during coffee breaks.

If your husband has a severe case of jealousy, however, your efforts will not be successful. You can take an oath that you'll never look at another man, you can even spit on men in front of your husband . . . nothing will work. The only thing you can do is tell yourself that jealousy is flattering.

Chapter 26

So What If You Wore the Same Thing Yesterday!

You don't need your makeup,
Your lipstick or comb
When you earn your money
By working at home.

For some women, being a wage earner means working at home. They work in the kid-bite-kid world rather than the dog-eat-dog world. This has its advantages. As one mother said, "I would rather find out first-hand that my kids are rotten than hear it from a sitter. Also, I can talk to myself and no one will think I'm weird."

But working at home also has its disadvantages. For instance, a quarrel between two co-workers is interesting, whereas a quarrel between your kids is upsetting. Also, when the toilet gets stopped up you can't send for the janitor.

If you're thinking of earning money by working at home, try some of these tips:

Have your newspaper delivered next door and pick it up in the evening. That way, you won't be tempted to sit down with a cup of coffee and the paper.

Even if the mailman is the only adult you'll see all day, don't lure him into a long conversation.

Throw a tarp over the breakfast table so you can get to work immediately.

Replace live flowers and plants with artificial ones. That way, you won't be tempted to water them as an excuse for avoiding work.

Install a smoke alarm because you'll be working while your dinner is in the oven. (Teach your kids to dial 911 in case you're concentrating so hard you don't hear it go off.)

If you're a writer, write children's books. You can't ask a five-year-old "How does this sound?" and read him an excerpt from a Harlequin romance.

Always keep a picture in front of you of the piece of furniture or appliance you are working to replace.

To cut down on visitors, put them to work.

Phone soliciting is a popular way to earn money at home, despite the fact that it guarantees verbal abuse. If you do this kind of work, tell people you're involved in telecommunications so it won't sound as brutish as it really is. These tips might help you in your work:

No matter how noisy your kids are, don't make your calls from a pay phone.

Even if you're desperate, don't put your child on the phone and have her say "Pretty please."

If a phone solicitor calls you, make *her* listen to *your* spiel.

Some women baby-sit to earn money while they take care of their own children. This has its problems too. For instance, writing an ad that reads "Will baby-sit in my neat, clean house" will not necessarily attract polite, considerate children. You can't charge kids a breakage fee, either. And remember, you're working to get ahead—so no matter how stressed you feel, don't bring *your* children to another sitter.

Even if you have only your own children to care for, make special rules for them so they don't interrupt you while you work. For instance, have them draw straws to see who is going to get your attention next, and set a designated tattling hour.

Your children may not follow your rules, however, so you'll have to manage them creatively. Suggestions like these could work for you:

The mucilage from envelopes may curb your kids' appetites.

Keep them dawdling over their breakfasts as long as possible.

Post a picture of kids fighting with a red diagonal line through it.

Teach at least one kid to tie snoes so he can tie for the rest of the family.

Have your kids help you lick envelopes. The mucilage may quell their appetites.

If their interruptions put your work behind schedule, make the kids apologize to your clients.

If a child is fussy, pretend he is the boss and you have to put up with him.

Women who work at home sometimes miss working with other adults. Granted, taking coffee breaks at home with your children is not as much fun as being in the lounge with co-workers. But then, co-workers often say nasty things behind your back. Your kids are more straightforward: they say nasty things to your face.

Chapter 27

Lifting Your Feet While I Vacuum Is Not Enough

How can you tell if
Your child's done the dishes?
He's spilled enough water
For three tanks of fishes.

Every working mother dreams of coming home to a sparkling house, a meal in the oven, and someone at the chopping board making salad. But this only happens when her mother or mother-in-law is visiting.

Having the husband do half the work around the house is a comparatively new idea that many men are still trying to quash. Even those who seem to accept this logical concept usually do not come close to doing their quota of one-half. In fact, one woman said "The only help my husband gives me with cleaning is letting me use his old T-shirts for dust rags."

Console yourself with these tales of the "assistance" husbands give their wives:

"He has the children take their baths on air mattresses so he won't have to scrub the bathtub."

"He poured the prize toy into the bowl with the cereal and Bradley broke a tooth."

"When I got home, he was having a tea party with Melissa and he had beer in his teacup."

"He shoehorned Nicky's size-five foot into Luke's size-three shoe."

"He used one of the kitchen curtains for a dishtowel."

"When the children misbehave, he sends them to me at work."

Husbands' and children's attention spans are equally short, and neither has a natural talent for housework. Moreover, persuading a reluctant husband to clean up can easily lead to a major fight. Work on your children instead.

Children can be good helpers if you know how to motivate them. Here are a few suggestions for capturing their imaginations:

If your children like history, tell them to pretend they're explorers and find new spots to clean where no man has ever been—like behind the refrigerator.

Let your children have a dustathon, a vacuumathon, or a mowathon. Limit the sponsors to yourself and your husband.

Have them draw a smile face instead of a check mark when they have completed the chore. This will put them in a better mood for the next chore.

Try to popularize HAVE YOU DONE YOUR CHORES FOR YOUR MOTHER TODAY? buttons.

Tell them a photographer from a national magazine is coming to your house.

Inform them that they must put their dirty clothes in the hamper themselves or they must teach the dog to do it.

Have a sign made for your child's room, like MATTHEW'S PAD. There's a chance he'll take enough pride in it to keep it clean.

Stamp your children's initials on scrubbing and dusting rags.

Make up cheers to yell, such as "Clean That House, Clean That House!" or "With an S, with a C, with an R-U-B!"

"Ooo-h" and "Ahhh-h" a lot when you inspect something they did well. Maybe you can get the dog to stand beside you and wag his tail.

Remind them that all the Waltons helped Mrs. Walton and she didn't even have a job outside the home.

As these examples plainly show, getting help from your family is one of your most difficult assignments. You will have to be creative, like the woman who used pizza-scented paper for the chore list. You may even have to wheedle, like the mother who wailed, "Can't we have just one day without dog hairs?" Most likely, however, you'll feel frustrated a lot of the time. By all means, preserve your dignity and sanity. If worst comes to worst, you can hang a sampler saying DULL WOMEN HAVE IMMACULATE HOMES.

Chapter 28

Come on in—Just Clear a Space and Sit Down

Once you would sweep
At the drop of a crumb.
Now that you're working,
Your house is a slum.

Even if you can persuade your family to pitch in on the housework, you'll have to come to terms with the fact that your house will be messier than it was when you were home during cleaning prime time.

Some silly souls argue that housekeeping is all a matter of organization. They say you can get just as much done around the house if you plan properly. These people are usually husbands who would like a little help paying the bills.

One way to reduce your work load is to stop doing anything that's not absolutely necessary. For example, by putting up a WE APPRECIATE YOUR NOT SMOKING sign, you can get out of emptying and washing ash trays. Also, if you make your ironing board into a plant stand, your family will no longer expect you to press anything.

Remember, however, that you will never have housework completely under control. Fatigue and lack of time will make you neglect the household, and things will soon deteriorate. If you see warning signals like these, intensify your efforts:

Your tabletops are so dusty, it looks like you have gray velvet doilies.

The water in the aquarium looks and smells like swamp water.

The only home-cooked meal served in your house all week was the baby's pablum.

You have twelve packs of 12-paks to be returned for deposit.

Your garage looks like the headquarters for the paper drive.

You can stage cushion-turnover drills and train your family to help in emergencies, but your best strategy is to convince people that you're a better housekeeper than you really are. Covering up won't be hard if you follow these suggestions:

Tape yourself vacuuming and play the tape often with the windows open.

Say that the apple cores and peach pits lying around are going to be sprayed for a craft project.

Buy your child enough stuffed animals to cover his unmade bed.

If you have a tattered or dirty sofa pillow, throw it on the floor when the doorbell rings. People will assume it belongs to the cat or dog.

If a guest gets dust or dirt in his eye, tell him it's an eyelash.

To make people think the dirt on the carpet just got there, yell "Who's tracking?!"

Buy your children enough stuffed animals to cover their unmade beds.

Make indentations with the vacuum cleaner so people will know you've vacuumed. To make them, say to one of your kids "Hop on, I'll give you a ride."

Leave a few party favors around as though you had just given a kids' birthday party.

If you put your mind to it, you can become a master of subterfuge. With a single sentence, you can convey the proper impression. For example, you can say "Excuse the mess, but if I clean it up myself the children will never learn."

Chapter 29

Do You Prefer the Crying or Non-crying Section of the Airplane?

When you're told
"Go home, get packed,"
Hit the road
Lest you get sacked.

Your life changes drastically when you take a trip for your company. One minute you're looking for a shoelace for your child's worn-out tennie and the next you're at an airport watching a businessman have his $250 shoes shined. Making the transition isn't easy, especially if you have small children. For example, you get in a rented car and automatically look for your child's car seat . . . until you realize the child is at home.

Whether you want to or not, you'll find yourself thinking about your children while you're traveling. You'll worry about them and think up ways to justify your trip. Of course, this makes your life even more difficult, but you can't help yourself.

When you find yourself in this predicament, try a few of these tips:

Call home at your kids' crabbiest time so you won't feel so bad about not being with them.

Try to make your children feel sorry for you instead of jealous. For example, explain a tan by saying

"They held one of the long, boring seminars outside in the motel courtyard."

Don't look at the empty bed in the motel room sadly. Instead, think "I don't have to stop my kids from jumping up and down on it."

Don't worry if you can't get out to buy your kids presents. You can always bring them the pen and notepad by the phone, soap and shower cap from the bathroom, or packages of crackers from the dining room.

Relieve some of your guilt by buying a parents' magazine instead of a gossip magazine at the airport.

Depending on how you use your time, a business trip can give you a lift or bring you down. Never rush off without preparation. For example, be sure the price tags are off your new clothes; you'll be embarrassed to ask a flight attendant for a

Some mothers just can't admit they'll enjoy a break from their families.

scissors. While you're away, don't address a postcard to the person at the office who would have gone on the trip if you hadn't been chosen, and don't ask her to put it on the bulletin board.

Dinner time can be especially trying. You might be so used to preparing and sharing meals that you'll have a hard time eating out while traveling. In fact, you could feel downright miserable. The hostess will ask "How many in your party?" but there's just you—definitely *not* a party. Your booth is so big and empty a burp echoes. The strolling violinist rolls his eyes heavenward as he passes your table.

You may not feel happy eating alone, but you might *appear* less lonely if you try some of these suggestions:

Look at your watch and say "Maybe I'd better go ahead and order."

Ask the waitress to bring you a phone book. She'll think you know someone in town. (You can count the number of Smiths and Joneses.)

When someone sneezes, don't say "God bless you!" if he is more than two tables away.

Sit near the kitchen. You might hear an interesting argument.

Don't pick up the vase on the table and sniff the flowers more than once.

If you're worried about leaving home, savor the advantages you'll have when traveling. For instance, think "I'*ll* get a wake-up call instead of giving one." And remember, a maid will make your bed.

In fact, you'll enjoy a break from your family. Don't pretend otherwise. A mother who says to her kids "I just wish I could pack you in my suitcase and take you with me" will lie about other things.

Try not to worry. Just give your last nosewipe and take off. Here's one word of caution, though: if you farm your kids out to different people, make sure to remember where you left each one.

Chapter 30

Sometimes It Isn't Great to Be a Mover

When your boss informs you
That you'll have to pack and move,
Don't expect your family
To holler "We approve!"

"We're living here because my husband's company transferred him" used to be a common statement. Today the cause of the relocation might just as easily be the woman's transfer.

Feminists have accomplished many things but they have not achieved the feat of having a husband readily accept his wife's move. Since there isn't much chance that your husband will be told on the same day that he is being transferred to the same city, you'd better put some thought into breaking the news. Here are a few suggestions:

Tell him on a Monday night when he isn't too thrilled about his own job.

Tell him you can get a bigger house and the kids will have a room of their own. (Unless you have to, don't add that if he won't move *he'll* have a room of his own.)

Tell him it's time he got his resumé updated and this would probably be the only way he would get around to it.

Wear a smile button when you tell him.

It's easier to convince your children that they won't mind moving. You can tell them that they'll get bigger ice cream cones in that city. If you have teenagers, tell them there is a better mall.

Of course, relocating *is* difficult, and you and your family are apt to feel so lonesome, even the telephone time lady will seem aloof.

One transferee was so desperate for friends she hung a welcome mat in her living-room window. Another woman cried at the sight of her old zip code. A husband complained to his wife, "Only one person asked me about myself today and that was a traffic cop who yelled, 'Where do you think *you're* going?!' "

Since moving is so traumatic, do everything you can to make a smooth adjustment. Here are a few hints for a sucessful relocation:

The relocation blues.

Unpack toothpaste and hand cream first, since your early days will be filled with smiling and shaking hands.

Never permit anyone in the family to use the word *uprooted*. Always say *relocated*.

If you think your family will be upset because you had to work late, tell them you got lost on the way home.

Listening to the morning weather forecast will not guarantee fascinating conversations, so you'll need other ways to make friends at work. Here are a few tips:

Join a car pool and offer to drive every day.

Contribute to all collections, even for flowers for the great-grandmother of someone who worked there fifteen years ago.

If co-workers aren't friendly, work late. Maybe the cleaning crew will talk to you.

Don't act too eager to make friends, like the woman who announced "My treat if anyone wants to go to lunch with me!"

Don't write your birthday on the community calendar the first week of your new job.

Keep a sewing kit in your desk. It's the equivalent of being able to play the piano at a party.

If your children make new friends fast and you don't, don't ask if you can go out with them.

Families often take a long time to adjust to a move, so be prepared to deal with resentment and loneliness. Anything that goes wrong the first couple of years will be blamed on you. During your first six months in a new city, you will have the urge to spend your coffee breaks on the playground with your weeping child.

All you can do to relieve the stress is go home and kick a packing box. However, be sure it's one you've emptied, since you could break your toe if it's full.

Chapter 31

I Think I'll Give My Notice

You know, I think it's time to quit:
I've got no time to read a book,
I never get my beauty sleep,
And I've forgotten how to cook.

What if you find that keeping up the house, resolving sitter hassles, meeting work deadlines, traveling, and laughing at the boss's unfunny jokes is more than you can take? Or maybe you just want to stay home and enjoy the things you've bought with your paychecks. How do you persuade your husband to agree that you needn't work?

The number of approaches is limited only by your imagination. For instance, you could argue that with all the insurance benefits you have from both jobs you aren't feeling enough pressure to keep your family well. Or you could say that the kids' college educations will mean more to them if they have to struggle to obtain them.

Chances are, however, your husband will be more receptive if you use arguments like these:

"You can complain about your work and I won't interrupt with problems of my own."

"My co-workers drive carelessly in the parking lot and the car is apt to get dented or scratched."

"If I don't have to get dressed for work in the morning, I'll be able to check if your tie is straight instead of looking to see if my slip is showing."

"I won't stop you when you tell a joke because I won't have heard it at work already."

Even if the children are happier with the sitter than with you, you can cite sitter problems. You can also place panty hose on top of the groceries to show him how expensive working is. But there are even better ways to convince your husband that your staying home will benefit him:

Remind him that you used to cook supper instead of just heating up canned food.

Tell him you'll have time to throw out all the junk mail before he sees it.

Tell him he won't have to keep saying "I must get my blood pressure checked" because you'll make his appointment.

Tell him you can get to Ticketron on time.

If you persevere, your husband just might agree that you should quit. On the day you actually do leave your job, be prepared with a clever announcement, such as "Jason needs a school bag and I told him he could have my briefcase."

But for you, quitting may only be a fantasy—like getting help with the housework. Do you really want to go back to "the days of whine and noses" anyhow? Think of the disadvantages of being at home instead of being in the work force. Here are a few:

You can't go to the bathroom alone.

Your family expects hot breakfasts and big dinners.

You have to wait until everyone else showers and you get cold water.

When you have a job, you can do exhilarating things like make out chore lists for your husband and children. You can eat lunch without worrying if the person sitting across from you is getting enough nutrition. And you don't have to fill in when other mothers' baby-sitters get sick.

THE BEST WEDDING SHOWER BOOK

by Courtney Cooke

The contemporary guide for planning wedding showers. Contains time- and money-saving ideas for decorating and food; innovative gifts; and fun, creative games! **$4.95**

Ordering #: 6059

THE BEST BABY SHOWER BOOK

by Courtney Cooke

Who says baby showers have to be dull? Finally, a contemporary guide for planning baby showers that's chock-full of helpful hints, recipes, decorating ideas and activities that are fun without being juvenile. **$4.95**

Ordering #: 1239

GETTING ORGANIZED FOR YOUR NEW BABY

by Maureen Bard

The fastest way to get organized for pregnancy, childbirth and new baby care. Busy expectant parents will love the checklists, forms, schedules, charts and hints because they make getting ready so much easier. **$4.95**

Ordering #: 1229

THE BEST BABY NAME BOOK

by Bruce Lansky

America's best-selling name book contains 13,000 up-to-date baby names. It's the most complete, helpful, entertaining and gifty baby name book on the market. **$3.95**

Ordering #: 1029

PRACTICAL PARENTING TIPS
by Vicki Lansky

The #1 selling tricks-of-the-trade book for new parents; tips on toilet training, discipline, travel, temper tantrums, child proofing and more. Spiral bound. **$6.95**
Ordering #: 1179

FEED ME! I'M YOURS
by Vicki Lansky

The best-selling guide to making fresh, pure baby foods at home; over 200 recipes; lists of finger, fun and birthday foods. Spiral bound. **$6.95**
Ordering #: 1109

DEAR BABYSITTER
by Vicki Lansky

Two sitter aids in one: a refillable 50-page instruction pad and a 48-page sitter's handbook with babysitting techniques, basic child care and first-aid information. Hard cover. **$8.95**
Ordering #: 1059

WHILE WE'RE OUT

This well-designed, inexpensive baby-sitter notebook features our charming cross-stitch design. This 48-page format has plenty of space for complete baby-sitter instructions plus space for permanent instructions and phone numbers inside the front cover. **$3.50**
Ordering #: 3230

DAVID, WE'RE PREGNANT!

by Lynn Johnston

101 laughing-out-loud cartoons about the humorous side of having a baby by the creator of the "For Better or Worse" comic strip. **$3.95**
Ordering #: 1049

HI MOM! HI DAD!

by Lynn Johnston

101 cartoons about the funny things that happen to parents of infants. **$3.95**
Ordering #: 1139

DO THEY EVER GROW UP?

by Lynn Johnston

A hilarious, 101-cartoon survival guide for parents of the tantrum and pre-school set. **$3.95**
Ordering #: 1089

MOTHER MURPHY'S LAW

by Bruce Lansky

The wit of Bombeck and the wisdom of Murphy are combined in this collection of 325 laws that detail the perils and pitfalls of parenthood. Cartoon illustrations by Christine Tripp. **$2.95**
Ordering #: 1149

GRANDMA KNOWS BEST BUT NO ONE EVER LISTENS

by Mary McBride

Mary McBride instructs grandmas who have been stuck with babysitting how to "scheme, lie, cheat, and threaten so you'll be thought of as a sweet, darling grandma." **$4.95**

Ordering #: 4009

LETTERS FROM A PREGNANT COWARD

by Joyce Armor

These hilarious letters from a terrified, over-anxious expectant mother to her parents, in-laws, siblings and friends express the fears and feelings that go along with being pregnant. Any woman and man who go through pregnancy will appreciate this collection of humorous insights. **$6.95**

Ordering #: 1289

HOW TO SURVIVE HIGH SCHOOL WITH MINIMAL BRAIN DAMAGE

by Doug Lansky and Aaron Dorfman

The hilarious guide for high school students that tells how to be cool in high school. It contains hundreds of pranks, hoaxes and dirty tricks. It's "the greatest invention for high school kids since Cliffs Notes."—Dave Barry. **$4.95**

Ordering #: 4050

MOTHER MURPHY'S 2nd LAW

by Bruce Lansky

A ribald collection of laws about love, sex, marriage and other skirmishes that can't be found in marriage or sex manuals. **$4.95**

Ordering #: 4010

WALL STREET BULL

by Bruce Lansky

The latest expose to rock Wall Street is a humorous lexicon of over 500 words commonly heard in Wall Street boardrooms and barrooms...and what they really mean. It exposes the gallows humor that lies at the heart of Wall Street bull. **$4.95**

Ordering #: 4040

LEXICON OF INTENTIONALLY AMBIGUOUS RECOMMENDATIONS (L.I.A.R.) *by Robert Thornton*

This witty guide can help you give a good recommendation to someone who can't manage his own sock drawer—and still tell the truth. Anyone who has ever had to write a recommendation needs this book. "Scathing condemnations that can be read as ringing praise."— Harry Reasoner, CBS News Broadcast. **$4.95**

Ordering #: 4070

FREE STUFF FOR KIDS

11th Edition

Over 250 free and up-to-a-dollar things kids can send for by mail. A classic children's activity book with over one million copies sold. It teaches kids the basics of letter writing and how to follow directions while at the same time providing them with fantastic offers. **$3.95**

Ordering #: 2190

WORDPLAY

by Charles Thiesen and Deanna King

A stimulating alternative to run-of-the-mill activity books that turns kids 8-14 into creative thinkers by: solving secret codes, making up wild stories, writing funny ads, inventing tongue-twisters, and more. Wordplay is so much fun, kids don't realize they're learning. **$5.95**

Ordering #: 2200

ORDER FORM

Qty.	Book Title	Author	Price
_____	Baby and Child Medical Care	Hart, T.	$5.95
_____	Baby Talk	Lansky, B.	$4.95
_____	Best Baby Name Book, The	Lansky, B.	$3.95
_____	Best Baby Shower Book, The	Cooke, C.	$4.95
_____	Best Wedding Shower Book, The	Cooke, C.	$4.95
_____	Birth Partner's Handbook, The	Simkin, P.	$4.95
_____	David, We're Pregnant!	Johnston, L.	$3.95
_____	Dear Babysitter	Lansky, V.	$8.95
_____	Discipline Without Shouting or Spanking	Wyckoff/Unell	$4.95
_____	Do They Ever Grow Up?	Johnston, L.	$3.95
_____	Exercises for Baby and Me	Regnier, S.	$9.95
_____	Feed Me! I'm Yours	Lansky, V.	$6.95
_____	First-Year Baby Care	Kelly, P.	$5.95
_____	Free Stuff for Kids	FSFK Editors	$3.95
_____	Getting Organized For Your New Baby	Bard, M.	$4.95
_____	Grandma Knows Best	McBride, M.	$4.95
_____	Hi Mom! Hi Dad!	Johnston, L.	$3.95
_____	How to Survive High School with minimal brain damage	Lansky/Dorfman . . .	$4.95
_____	Letters From a Pregnant Coward	Armor, J.	$6.95
_____	Lexicon of Intentionally Ambiguous Recommendations	Thornton, R.	$4.95
_____	Mother Murphy's Law	Lansky, B.	$2.95
_____	Mother Murphy's 2nd Law	Lansky, B.	$2.95
_____	Mother's Memories	Meadowbrook	$5.95
_____	Practical Parenting Tips	Lansky, V.	$6.95
_____	Pregnancy, Childbirth and the Newborn	Simkin/Whalley	$9.95
_____	Successful Breastfeeding	Dana/Price	$8.95
_____	Successful Single Parenting	Wayman, A.	$4.95
_____	Wall Street Bull	Lansky, B.	$4.95
_____	Webster's Dictionary Game	Webster, W.	$5.95
_____	While We're Out	Meadowbrook	$3.50
_____	Wordplay	Thiesen, C.	$5.95
_____	Working Woman's Guide to Breastfeeding, The . . .	Dana/Price	$5.95

Please send me copies of the books checked above. I am enclosing $_____
which covers the full amount per book shown above plus $1.25 for postage and handling for the first
book and $.50 for each additional book. (Add $2.00 to total for postage and handling for books shipped
to Canada. Overseas postage and handling will be billed. MN residents add 6% sales tax.) Allow up to
four weeks for delivery. **Quantity discounts available upon request.**

Send check or money order to Meadowbrook, Inc. No cash or C.O.D.s, please.

**For purchases over $10.00 you may use VISA or MasterCard (order by mail or phone). For these
orders we need information below.**

Charge to: ☐ VISA ☐ MasterCard   Account #_____

Expiration Date_____

Card Signature_____

Send Book(s) to:

Name_____

Address_____

City_____State_____Zip_____

**Mail order to: Book Orders, Meadowbrook, Inc., 18318 Minnetonka Blvd., Deephaven, MN 55391,
Phone orders. Toll Free (800) 338-2232.**